PRETTY SIMPLE

Stay Positive

A POSITIVITY JOURNAL

Scan this code for a special message from the Pretty Simple Press Team!

PLUS FREE BONUS!

Please email katie@paperpeonypress.com if you're having trouble with the code.

Stay Positive: A Positivity Journal
© Paper Peony Press.

Published by: Paper Peony Press
www.paperpeonypress.com

All rights reserved. *Stay Positive: A Positivity Journal* is under copyright protection. No part of this journal may be used or reproduced in any manner whatsoever without written permission except in the case of brief quotations embodied in critical articles and reviews.

For wholesale inquiries contact: reagan@paperpeonypress.com

WELCOME TO THE POSITIVITY JOURNAL

Positivity (*noun*) : the practice of being positive and hopeful in demeanor and attitude.

When we think about positivity, we often think of an attitude that some of us possess by nature and others do not. By definition, however, positivity is a practice. A skill that is within reach of each and every one of us if we dedicate time to practice more of it.

This book isn't going to give you a magic formula to becoming a more positive and joyful person. We have no secret list of 10 routines to a happier life and it is most certainly not designed to create perfection in this area of your life. It is about starting each day with a fresh outlook and ending each day in quiet reflection. It is space to start a new practice of positivity. Take note of the good. Celebrate it. Reflect on it.

We're cheering you on. Stay positive.

30 DAY MINDFULNESS CHALLENGE

Track your mood with this chart as you go through the first 30 days of this challenge. Once you have completed all 30 days, come back here and review the overall mood you experienced during this time. What are some specific events from the hard days that may have triggered feelings of anger, frustration, sadness, or anxiety? What are some triggers that brought joy to the good days?

Being mindful of the things we do and do not allow into our days has immense power to shape our overall positivity!

POSITIVE TRIGGERS:

NEGATIVE TRIGGERS:

KEY

- happy & joyful
- excited
- confused
- calm & content
- frustrated/angry
- anxious
- sad
- other (write in your own)

Imagine what's possible.

	☀	✎	?	☁	🔥	🔍	💧	OTHER
01								
02								
03								
04								
05								
06								
07								
08								
09								
10								
11								
12								
13								
14								
15								
16								
17								
18								
19								
20								
21								
22								
23								
24								
25								
26								
27								
28								
29								
30								

FEEL GOOD GOALS

Here is a place for you to jot down all your big picture goals. What do you hope to accomplish during your 60 days of positivity? Dream big, this space is just for you!

Goal #1

Goal #2

Goal #3

Goal #4

Goal #5

PICK-ME-UPS

Take some time to think through the things that make you smile and list them out below. When you're feeling down, flip back to this page and pick a fun activity to do. There is always joy to be found, sometimes you just have to train yourself to find it!

Places to visit:
- ○ _____
- ○ _____
- ○ _____
- ○ _____
- ○ _____

Movies to watch:
- ○ _____
- ○ _____
- ○ _____
- ○ _____
- ○ _____

Books to read:
- ○ _____
- ○ _____
- ○ _____
- ○ _____
- ○ _____

Friends to call:
- ○ _____
- ○ _____
- ○ _____
- ○ _____
- ○ _____

Food to eat:
- ○ _____
- ○ _____
- ○ _____
- ○ _____
- ○ _____

Outdoor activity:
- ○ _____
- ○ _____
- ○ _____
- ○ _____
- ○ _____

Meals to cook:

-
-
-
-
-

Sights to see:

-
-
-
-
-

Guilty Pleasures:

-
-
-
-
-

Smells that take you back:

-
-
-
-
-

Songs to listen to:

-
-
-
-
-

-
-
-
-
-

You've set your intentions and made your lists...
now let's get to practicing positivity!
Happy journaling!

day 01

POSITIVE INTENTION
Write down your positive affirmation for today.

CURRENT FEELINGS

CHOSEN FEELINGS

WHAT ARE YOU LOOKING FORWARD TO?

GOALS

I AM GRATEFUL FOR...

1. _____
2. _____
3. _____

Evening ☾   M   D   Y

OVERALL, TODAY FELT

THREE THINGS THAT WENT WELL TODAY:

1. _____

2. _____

3. _____

HIGHLIGHT OF THE DAY

STANDOUT HUMAN OF THE DAY

SET UP FOR SUCCESS TOMORROW

day 02

POSITIVE INTENTION
Write down your positive affirmation for today.

CURRENT FEELINGS

CHOSEN FEELINGS

WHAT ARE YOU LOOKING FORWARD TO?

GOALS

I AM GRATEFUL FOR...

1. _____
2. _____
3. _____

Evening ☾   M   D   Y

OVERALL, TODAY FELT

THREE THINGS THAT WENT WELL TODAY:

1. _____
2. _____
3. _____

HIGHLIGHT OF THE DAY

STANDOUT HUMAN OF THE DAY

SET UP FOR SUCCESS TOMORROW

day 03

POSITIVE INTENTION
Write down your positive affirmation for today.

CURRENT FEELINGS

CHOSEN FEELINGS

WHAT ARE YOU LOOKING FORWARD TO?

GOALS

I AM GRATEFUL FOR...

1.
2.
3.

Evening ☾

M　　D　　Y.

OVERALL, TODAY FELT

THREE THINGS THAT WENT WELL TODAY:

1. _____
2. _____
3. _____

HIGHLIGHT OF THE DAY

STANDOUT HUMAN OF THE DAY

SET UP FOR SUCCESS TOMORROW

day 04

POSITIVE INTENTION
Write down your positive affirmation for today.

CURRENT FEELINGS

CHOSEN FEELINGS

WHAT ARE YOU LOOKING FORWARD TO?

GOALS

I AM GRATEFUL FOR...
1.
2.
3.

Evening ☾   M   D   Y

OVERALL, TODAY FELT

THREE THINGS THAT WENT WELL TODAY:

1. _____

2. _____

3. _____

HIGHLIGHT OF THE DAY

STANDOUT HUMAN OF THE DAY

SET UP FOR SUCCESS TOMORROW

day 05 ☼ **Morning**

POSITIVE INTENTION
Write down your positive affirmation for today.

CURRENT FEELINGS

CHOSEN FEELINGS

WHAT ARE YOU LOOKING FORWARD TO?

GOALS

I AM GRATEFUL FOR...

1.

2.

3.

Evening ☾

M   D   Y

OVERALL, TODAY FELT

THREE THINGS THAT WENT WELL TODAY:

1.
2.
3.

HIGHLIGHT OF THE DAY

STANDOUT HUMAN OF THE DAY

SET UP FOR SUCCESS TOMORROW

day 06

POSITIVE INTENTION
Write down your positive affirmation for today.

CURRENT FEELINGS

CHOSEN FEELINGS

WHAT ARE YOU LOOKING FORWARD TO?

GOALS

I AM GRATEFUL FOR...

1.
2.
3.

Evening ☾   M   D   Y

OVERALL, TODAY FELT

___

THREE THINGS THAT WENT WELL TODAY:

1. ___
2. ___
3. ___

HIGHLIGHT OF THE DAY

___

STANDOUT HUMAN OF THE DAY

___

SET UP FOR SUCCESS TOMORROW

day 07

POSITIVE INTENTION
Write down your positive affirmation for today.

CURRENT FEELINGS   CHOSEN FEELINGS

WHAT ARE YOU LOOKING FORWARD TO?

GOALS

I AM GRATEFUL FOR...

1.
2.
3.

Evening ☾   M   D   Y

OVERALL, TODAY FELT

THREE THINGS THAT WENT WELL TODAY:

1.
2.
3.

HIGHLIGHT OF THE DAY

STANDOUT HUMAN OF THE DAY

SET UP FOR SUCCESS TOMORROW

day 08

POSITIVE INTENTION
Write down your positive affirmation for today.

CURRENT FEELINGS

CHOSEN FEELINGS

WHAT ARE YOU LOOKING FORWARD TO?

GOALS

I AM GRATEFUL FOR...

1.
2.
3.

Evening ☾   M   D   Y

OVERALL, TODAY FELT

THREE THINGS THAT WENT WELL TODAY:

1.
2.
3.

HIGHLIGHT OF THE DAY

STANDOUT HUMAN OF THE DAY

SET UP FOR SUCCESS TOMORROW

day 09

 **Morning**

POSITIVE INTENTION
Write down your positive affirmation for today.

CURRENT FEELINGS

CHOSEN FEELINGS

WHAT ARE YOU LOOKING FORWARD TO?

GOALS

I AM GRATEFUL FOR...

1.
2.
3.

Evening ☾

M   D   Y

OVERALL, TODAY FELT

THREE THINGS THAT WENT WELL TODAY:

1.
2.
3.

HIGHLIGHT OF THE DAY

STANDOUT HUMAN OF THE DAY

SET UP FOR SUCCESS TOMORROW

day 10

 **Morning**

POSITIVE INTENTION
Write down your positive affirmation for today.

CURRENT FEELINGS

CHOSEN FEELINGS

WHAT ARE YOU LOOKING FORWARD TO?

GOALS

I AM GRATEFUL FOR…

1.
2.
3.

Evening ☾

M   D   Y

OVERALL, TODAY FELT

THREE THINGS THAT WENT WELL TODAY:

1.
2.
3.

HIGHLIGHT OF THE DAY

STANDOUT HUMAN OF THE DAY

SET UP FOR SUCCESS TOMORROW

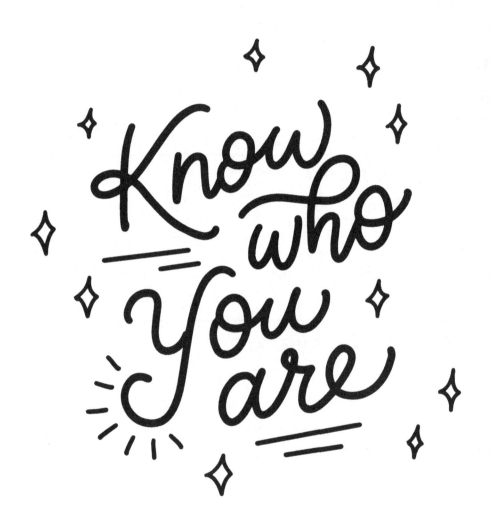

[AND WHAT MAKES YOU HAPPY]

POSITIVITY CHALLENGE *no. 1*

RE-WATCH A FILM YOU LOVE WHILE EATING ONE OF YOUR FAVORITE FOODS.

Write about your experience below

DATE COMPLETED	/ /

day 11 ☼ **Morning**

POSITIVE INTENTION
Write down your positive affirmation for today.

CURRENT FEELINGS

CHOSEN FEELINGS

WHAT ARE YOU LOOKING FORWARD TO?

GOALS

I AM GRATEFUL FOR...

1. _____
2. _____
3. _____

Evening ☾

M D Y

OVERALL, TODAY FELT

THREE THINGS THAT WENT WELL TODAY:

1. _____
2. _____
3. _____

HIGHLIGHT OF THE DAY

STANDOUT HUMAN OF THE DAY

SET UP FOR SUCCESS TOMORROW

day 12

POSITIVE INTENTION
Write down your positive affirmation for today.

CURRENT FEELINGS   CHOSEN FEELINGS

WHAT ARE YOU LOOKING FORWARD TO?

GOALS

I AM GRATEFUL FOR...
1. ___
2. ___
3. ___

Evening ☾

M   D   Y

OVERALL, TODAY FELT

THREE THINGS THAT WENT WELL TODAY:

1. _____

2. _____

3. _____

HIGHLIGHT OF THE DAY

STANDOUT HUMAN OF THE DAY

SET UP FOR SUCCESS TOMORROW

day 13

POSITIVE INTENTION
Write down your positive affirmation for today.

CURRENT FEELINGS

CHOSEN FEELINGS

WHAT ARE YOU LOOKING FORWARD TO?

GOALS

I AM GRATEFUL FOR...

1.
2.
3.

Evening ☾

M   D   Y

OVERALL, TODAY FELT

THREE THINGS THAT WENT WELL TODAY:

1. _____

2. _____

3. _____

HIGHLIGHT OF THE DAY

STANDOUT HUMAN OF THE DAY

SET UP FOR SUCCESS TOMORROW

day 14

 **Morning**

POSITIVE INTENTION
Write down your positive affirmation for today.

CURRENT FEELINGS

CHOSEN FEELINGS

WHAT ARE YOU LOOKING FORWARD TO?

GOALS

I AM GRATEFUL FOR...

1.

2.

3.

Evening ☾

M　　D　　Y

OVERALL, TODAY FELT

THREE THINGS THAT WENT WELL TODAY:

1. _____

2. _____

3. _____

HIGHLIGHT OF THE DAY

_____
_____
_____
_____

STANDOUT HUMAN OF THE DAY

_____
_____

SET UP FOR SUCCESS TOMORROW

day 15

☼ **Morning**

POSITIVE INTENTION
Write down your positive affirmation for today.

CURRENT FEELINGS

CHOSEN FEELINGS

WHAT ARE YOU LOOKING FORWARD TO?

GOALS

I AM GRATEFUL FOR...

1.
2.
3.

Evening ☾   M   D   Y

OVERALL, TODAY FELT

THREE THINGS THAT WENT WELL TODAY:

1. _____

2. _____

3. _____

HIGHLIGHT OF THE DAY

STANDOUT HUMAN OF THE DAY

SET UP FOR SUCCESS TOMORROW

day 16 ☀ **Morning**

POSITIVE INTENTION
Write down your positive affirmation for today.

CURRENT FEELINGS

CHOSEN FEELINGS

WHAT ARE YOU LOOKING FORWARD TO?

GOALS

I AM GRATEFUL FOR...

1.

2.

3.

Evening ☾   M   D   Y

OVERALL, TODAY FELT

THREE THINGS THAT WENT WELL TODAY:

1.

2.

3.

HIGHLIGHT OF THE DAY

STANDOUT HUMAN OF THE DAY

SET UP FOR SUCCESS TOMORROW

day 17

POSITIVE INTENTION
Write down your positive affirmation for today.

CURRENT FEELINGS

CHOSEN FEELINGS

WHAT ARE YOU LOOKING FORWARD TO?

GOALS

I AM GRATEFUL FOR...

1.
2.
3.

Evening ☾   M   D   Y

OVERALL, TODAY FELT

THREE THINGS THAT WENT WELL TODAY:

1.
2.
3.

HIGHLIGHT OF THE DAY

STANDOUT HUMAN OF THE DAY

SET UP FOR SUCCESS TOMORROW

day 18

 **Morning**

POSITIVE INTENTION
Write down your positive affirmation for today.

CURRENT FEELINGS

CHOSEN FEELINGS

WHAT ARE YOU LOOKING FORWARD TO?

GOALS

I AM GRATEFUL FOR...

1.
2.
3.

Evening ☾   M   D   Y

OVERALL, TODAY FELT

THREE THINGS THAT WENT WELL TODAY:

1. _____

2. _____

3. _____

HIGHLIGHT OF THE DAY

STANDOUT HUMAN OF THE DAY

SET UP FOR SUCCESS TOMORROW

day 19

 **Morning**

POSITIVE INTENTION
Write down your positive affirmation for today.

CURRENT FEELINGS

CHOSEN FEELINGS

WHAT ARE YOU LOOKING FORWARD TO?

GOALS

I AM GRATEFUL FOR...

1.

2.

3.

Evening ☾

M   D   Y

OVERALL, TODAY FELT

THREE THINGS THAT WENT WELL TODAY:

1. _____
2. _____
3. _____

HIGHLIGHT OF THE DAY

STANDOUT HUMAN OF THE DAY

SET UP FOR SUCCESS TOMORROW

day 20

POSITIVE INTENTION
Write down your positive affirmation for today.

CURRENT FEELINGS

CHOSEN FEELINGS

WHAT ARE YOU LOOKING FORWARD TO?

GOALS

I AM GRATEFUL FOR...

1.
2.
3.

Evening ☾

M   D   Y

OVERALL, TODAY FELT

THREE THINGS THAT WENT WELL TODAY:

1. _____

2. _____

3. _____

HIGHLIGHT OF THE DAY

STANDOUT HUMAN OF THE DAY

SET UP FOR SUCCESS TOMORROW

POSITIVITY CHALLENGE   *no. 2*

THINK ABOUT A TIME YOU'VE CRIED WITH LAUGHTER.

Does the mere memory of it bring a smile to your face? Write about it below.

DATE COMPLETED	/ /

day 21

POSITIVE INTENTION
Write down your positive affirmation for today.

CURRENT FEELINGS

CHOSEN FEELINGS

WHAT ARE YOU LOOKING FORWARD TO?

GOALS

I AM GRATEFUL FOR...

1.
2.
3.

Evening ☾　　　　　M　D　Y

OVERALL, TODAY FELT

_____

THREE THINGS THAT WENT WELL TODAY:

1. _____

2. _____

3. _____

HIGHLIGHT OF THE DAY

_____
_____
_____
_____

STANDOUT HUMAN OF THE DAY

_____
_____

SET UP FOR SUCCESS TOMORROW

day 22

POSITIVE INTENTION
Write down your positive affirmation for today.

CURRENT FEELINGS

CHOSEN FEELINGS

WHAT ARE YOU LOOKING FORWARD TO?

GOALS

I AM GRATEFUL FOR...

1. _____
2. _____
3. _____

Evening ☾

M   D   Y

OVERALL, TODAY FELT

THREE THINGS THAT WENT WELL TODAY:

1. _____

2. _____

3. _____

HIGHLIGHT OF THE DAY

STANDOUT HUMAN OF THE DAY

SET UP FOR SUCCESS TOMORROW

day 23

POSITIVE INTENTION
Write down your positive affirmation for today.

CURRENT FEELINGS

CHOSEN FEELINGS

WHAT ARE YOU LOOKING FORWARD TO?

GOALS

I AM GRATEFUL FOR...

1.
2.
3.

Evening ☾   M   D   Y

OVERALL, TODAY FELT

THREE THINGS THAT WENT WELL TODAY:

1. _____

2. _____

3. _____

HIGHLIGHT OF THE DAY

STANDOUT HUMAN OF THE DAY

SET UP FOR SUCCESS TOMORROW

day 24　　　　　　　　　　　　　　　　　　　　　☼ **Morning**

POSITIVE INTENTION
Write down your positive affirmation for today.

CURRENT FEELINGS　　　　　　## CHOSEN FEELINGS

_____　　　　_____

_____　　　　_____

_____　　　　_____

WHAT ARE YOU LOOKING FORWARD TO?

_____

_____

_____

_____

GOALS

_____

_____

_____

_____

I AM GRATEFUL FOR...

1. _____

2. _____

3. _____

Evening ☾   M   D   Y

OVERALL, TODAY FELT

_____

THREE THINGS THAT WENT WELL TODAY:

1. _____

2. _____

3. _____

HIGHLIGHT OF THE DAY

_____
_____
_____
_____

STANDOUT HUMAN OF THE DAY

_____
_____

SET UP FOR SUCCESS TOMORROW

day 25 ☼ **Morning**

POSITIVE INTENTION
Write down your positive affirmation for today.

CURRENT FEELINGS

CHOSEN FEELINGS

WHAT ARE YOU LOOKING FORWARD TO?

GOALS

I AM GRATEFUL FOR...

1.
2.
3.

Evening ☾ M D Y

OVERALL, TODAY FELT

THREE THINGS THAT WENT WELL TODAY:

1. _____

2. _____

3. _____

HIGHLIGHT OF THE DAY

STANDOUT HUMAN OF THE DAY

SET UP FOR SUCCESS TOMORROW

day 26

POSITIVE INTENTION
Write down your positive affirmation for today.

CURRENT FEELINGS

CHOSEN FEELINGS

WHAT ARE YOU LOOKING FORWARD TO?

GOALS

I AM GRATEFUL FOR...

1.
2.
3.

Evening ☾   M   D   Y

OVERALL, TODAY FELT

THREE THINGS THAT WENT WELL TODAY:

1.

2.

3.

HIGHLIGHT OF THE DAY

STANDOUT HUMAN OF THE DAY

SET UP FOR SUCCESS TOMORROW

day 27

POSITIVE INTENTION
Write down your positive affirmation for today.

CURRENT FEELINGS

CHOSEN FEELINGS

WHAT ARE YOU LOOKING FORWARD TO?

GOALS

I AM GRATEFUL FOR...

1. _____

2. _____

3. _____

Evening ☾   M   D   Y

OVERALL, TODAY FELT

THREE THINGS THAT WENT WELL TODAY:

1. _____

2. _____

3. _____

HIGHLIGHT OF THE DAY

STANDOUT HUMAN OF THE DAY

SET UP FOR SUCCESS TOMORROW

day 28

POSITIVE INTENTION
Write down your positive affirmation for today.

CURRENT FEELINGS

CHOSEN FEELINGS

WHAT ARE YOU LOOKING FORWARD TO?

GOALS

I AM GRATEFUL FOR...

1.
2.
3.

Evening ☾

M   D   Y

OVERALL, TODAY FELT

THREE THINGS THAT WENT WELL TODAY:

1.

2.

3.

HIGHLIGHT OF THE DAY

STANDOUT HUMAN OF THE DAY

SET UP FOR SUCCESS TOMORROW

day 29

POSITIVE INTENTION
Write down your positive affirmation for today.

CURRENT FEELINGS

CHOSEN FEELINGS

WHAT ARE YOU LOOKING FORWARD TO?

GOALS

I AM GRATEFUL FOR...

1.
2.
3.

Evening ☾

M   D   Y

OVERALL, TODAY FELT

THREE THINGS THAT WENT WELL TODAY:

1.
2.
3.

HIGHLIGHT OF THE DAY

STANDOUT HUMAN OF THE DAY

SET UP FOR SUCCESS TOMORROW

day 30

 **Morning**

POSITIVE INTENTION

Write down your positive affirmation for today.

CURRENT FEELINGS

CHOSEN FEELINGS

WHAT ARE YOU LOOKING FORWARD TO?

GOALS

I AM GRATEFUL FOR...

1. _____
2. _____
3. _____

Evening ☾

M   D   Y

OVERALL, TODAY FELT

THREE THINGS THAT WENT WELL TODAY:

1. _____

2. _____

3. _____

HIGHLIGHT OF THE DAY

STANDOUT HUMAN OF THE DAY

SET UP FOR SUCCESS TOMORROW

POSITIVITY CHALLENGE *no. 3*

WRITE A LETTER TO YOURSELF.

Write a letter to tell your future self about some of your biggest hopes and dreams for your life. Use the space below or seal a letter in an envelope to open at a later date when you may need some encouragement. The more we dream, the more hope we have and hope always gives way to positivity!

DATE COMPLETED	/ /

30 DAY MOOD TRACKER

30 days down, way to go! Use this chart to track the next 30 days. Remember to stay mindful of both the positive and negative triggers in your life.

KEY —————————————— happy & joyful 🙂
excited 😃
confused 😕
calm & content 😌
frustrated/angry 😠
anxious 😰
sad 😢
other (write in your own) ⚪

	😊	😃	😕	🙂	😣	😟	😦	OTHER
01								
02								
03								
04								
05								
06								
07								
08								
09								
10								
11								
12								
13								
14								
15								
16								
17								
18								
19								
20								
21								
22								
23								
24								
25								
26								
27								
28								
29								
30								

day 31

POSITIVE INTENTION
Write down your positive affirmation for today.

CURRENT FEELINGS

CHOSEN FEELINGS

WHAT ARE YOU LOOKING FORWARD TO?

GOALS

I AM GRATEFUL FOR...

1.
2.
3.

Evening ☾   M   D   Y

OVERALL, TODAY FELT

THREE THINGS THAT WENT WELL TODAY:

1.

2.

3.

HIGHLIGHT OF THE DAY

STANDOUT HUMAN OF THE DAY

SET UP FOR SUCCESS TOMORROW

day 32

POSITIVE INTENTION
Write down your positive affirmation for today.

CURRENT FEELINGS	CHOSEN FEELINGS

WHAT ARE YOU LOOKING FORWARD TO?

GOALS

I AM GRATEFUL FOR...

1.
2.
3.

Evening ☾

M   D   Y

OVERALL, TODAY FELT

THREE THINGS THAT WENT WELL TODAY:

1. _____
2. _____
3. _____

HIGHLIGHT OF THE DAY

STANDOUT HUMAN OF THE DAY

SET UP FOR SUCCESS TOMORROW

day 33

POSITIVE INTENTION
Write down your positive affirmation for today.

CURRENT FEELINGS

CHOSEN FEELINGS

WHAT ARE YOU LOOKING FORWARD TO?

GOALS

I AM GRATEFUL FOR…

1.
2.
3.

Evening ☾   M   D   Y

OVERALL, TODAY FELT

THREE THINGS THAT WENT WELL TODAY:

1. _____

2. _____

3. _____

HIGHLIGHT OF THE DAY

STANDOUT HUMAN OF THE DAY

SET UP FOR SUCCESS TOMORROW

day 34

 **Morning**

POSITIVE INTENTION
Write down your positive affirmation for today.

CURRENT FEELINGS

CHOSEN FEELINGS

WHAT ARE YOU LOOKING FORWARD TO?

GOALS

I AM GRATEFUL FOR...

1.
2.
3.

Evening ☾

M   D   Y

OVERALL, TODAY FELT

THREE THINGS THAT WENT WELL TODAY:

1.

2.

3.

HIGHLIGHT OF THE DAY

STANDOUT HUMAN OF THE DAY

SET UP FOR SUCCESS TOMORROW

day 35

POSITIVE INTENTION
Write down your positive affirmation for today.

CURRENT FEELINGS

CHOSEN FEELINGS

WHAT ARE YOU LOOKING FORWARD TO?

GOALS

I AM GRATEFUL FOR...
1.
2.
3.

Evening ☾

M   D   Y

OVERALL, TODAY FELT

THREE THINGS THAT WENT WELL TODAY:

1. _____

2. _____

3. _____

HIGHLIGHT OF THE DAY

STANDOUT HUMAN OF THE DAY

SET UP FOR SUCCESS TOMORROW

day 36

POSITIVE INTENTION
Write down your positive affirmation for today.

CURRENT FEELINGS

CHOSEN FEELINGS

WHAT ARE YOU LOOKING FORWARD TO?

GOALS

I AM GRATEFUL FOR...

1.
2.
3.

Evening ☾

M   D   Y

OVERALL, TODAY FELT

THREE THINGS THAT WENT WELL TODAY:

1.
2.
3.

HIGHLIGHT OF THE DAY

STANDOUT HUMAN OF THE DAY

SET UP FOR SUCCESS TOMORROW

day 37

POSITIVE INTENTION
Write down your positive affirmation for today.

CURRENT FEELINGS

CHOSEN FEELINGS

WHAT ARE YOU LOOKING FORWARD TO?

GOALS

I AM GRATEFUL FOR...

1.
2.
3.

Evening ☾   M   D   Y

OVERALL, TODAY FELT

THREE THINGS THAT WENT WELL TODAY:

1.

2.

3.

HIGHLIGHT OF THE DAY

STANDOUT HUMAN OF THE DAY

SET UP FOR SUCCESS TOMORROW

day 38

POSITIVE INTENTION
Write down your positive affirmation for today.

CURRENT FEELINGS

CHOSEN FEELINGS

WHAT ARE YOU LOOKING FORWARD TO?

GOALS

I AM GRATEFUL FOR...

1.
2.
3.

Evening ☾

M　D　Y

OVERALL, TODAY FELT

THREE THINGS THAT WENT WELL TODAY:

1.

2.

3.

HIGHLIGHT OF THE DAY

STANDOUT HUMAN OF THE DAY

SET UP FOR SUCCESS TOMORROW

day 39

POSITIVE INTENTION
Write down your positive affirmation for today.

CURRENT FEELINGS

CHOSEN FEELINGS

WHAT ARE YOU LOOKING FORWARD TO?

GOALS

I AM GRATEFUL FOR...

1.
2.
3.

Evening ☾

M   D   Y

OVERALL, TODAY FELT

THREE THINGS THAT WENT WELL TODAY:

1.
2.
3.

HIGHLIGHT OF THE DAY

STANDOUT HUMAN OF THE DAY

SET UP FOR SUCCESS TOMORROW

day 40 ☼ **Morning**

POSITIVE INTENTION
Write down your positive affirmation for today.

CURRENT FEELINGS   CHOSEN FEELINGS

_____   _____

_____   _____

_____   _____

WHAT ARE YOU LOOKING FORWARD TO?

_____

_____

_____

_____

GOALS

_____

_____

_____

_____

I AM GRATEFUL FOR...

1. _____

2. _____

3. _____

Evening ☾

M   D   Y

OVERALL, TODAY FELT

THREE THINGS THAT WENT WELL TODAY:

1. _____

2. _____

3. _____

HIGHLIGHT OF THE DAY

STANDOUT HUMAN OF THE DAY

SET UP FOR SUCCESS TOMORROW

POSITIVITY CHALLENGE   *no. 4*

WATCH THE SUNSET TODAY.

Soak in today for exactly what it is. The colors in the sky, the patterns of the clouds are specifically unique to this day alone. Reflect on the importance of being present in this current moment.

DATE COMPLETED	/ /

day 41    **Morning**

POSITIVE INTENTION
Write down your positive affirmation for today.

CURRENT FEELINGS   CHOSEN FEELINGS

WHAT ARE YOU LOOKING FORWARD TO?

GOALS

I AM GRATEFUL FOR...

1.
2.
3.

Evening ☾

M　　D　　Y

OVERALL, TODAY FELT

THREE THINGS THAT WENT WELL TODAY:

1.
2.
3.

HIGHLIGHT OF THE DAY

STANDOUT HUMAN OF THE DAY

SET UP FOR SUCCESS TOMORROW

day 42

POSITIVE INTENTION
Write down your positive affirmation for today.

CURRENT FEELINGS

CHOSEN FEELINGS

WHAT ARE YOU LOOKING FORWARD TO?

GOALS

I AM GRATEFUL FOR...

1.
2.
3.

Evening ☾   M   D   Y

OVERALL, TODAY FELT

_____

THREE THINGS THAT WENT WELL TODAY:

1. _____
2. _____
3. _____

HIGHLIGHT OF THE DAY

_____
_____
_____
_____
_____

STANDOUT HUMAN OF THE DAY

_____
_____

SET UP FOR SUCCESS TOMORROW

day 43

POSITIVE INTENTION
Write down your positive affirmation for today.

CURRENT FEELINGS

CHOSEN FEELINGS

WHAT ARE YOU LOOKING FORWARD TO?

GOALS

I AM GRATEFUL FOR...

1.
2.
3.

Evening ☾　　　　　　M　　D　　Y

OVERALL, TODAY FELT

THREE THINGS THAT WENT WELL TODAY:

1. _____

2. _____

3. _____

HIGHLIGHT OF THE DAY

STANDOUT HUMAN OF THE DAY

SET UP FOR SUCCESS TOMORROW

day 44

POSITIVE INTENTION
Write down your positive affirmation for today.

CURRENT FEELINGS

CHOSEN FEELINGS

WHAT ARE YOU LOOKING FORWARD TO?

GOALS

I AM GRATEFUL FOR...

1.
2.
3.

Evening ☾　　　　　　　　M　　D　　Y

OVERALL, TODAY FELT

THREE THINGS THAT WENT WELL TODAY:

1.

2.

3.

HIGHLIGHT OF THE DAY

STANDOUT HUMAN OF THE DAY

SET UP FOR SUCCESS TOMORROW

day 45 ☀ **Morning**

POSITIVE INTENTION
Write down your positive affirmation for today.

CURRENT FEELINGS   CHOSEN FEELINGS

WHAT ARE YOU LOOKING FORWARD TO?

GOALS

I AM GRATEFUL FOR...

1.
2.
3.

Evening ☾

M   D   Y

OVERALL, TODAY FELT

THREE THINGS THAT WENT WELL TODAY:

1.
2.
3.

HIGHLIGHT OF THE DAY

STANDOUT HUMAN OF THE DAY

SET UP FOR SUCCESS TOMORROW

day 46

POSITIVE INTENTION
Write down your positive affirmation for today.

CURRENT FEELINGS

CHOSEN FEELINGS

WHAT ARE YOU LOOKING FORWARD TO?

GOALS

I AM GRATEFUL FOR...

1.
2.
3.

Evening ☾

M   D   Y

OVERALL, TODAY FELT

THREE THINGS THAT WENT WELL TODAY:

1.

2.

3.

HIGHLIGHT OF THE DAY

STANDOUT HUMAN OF THE DAY

SET UP FOR SUCCESS TOMORROW

day 47

POSITIVE INTENTION
Write down your positive affirmation for today.

CURRENT FEELINGS

CHOSEN FEELINGS

WHAT ARE YOU LOOKING FORWARD TO?

GOALS

I AM GRATEFUL FOR...

1.
2.
3.

Evening ☾

M   D   Y

OVERALL, TODAY FELT

THREE THINGS THAT WENT WELL TODAY:

1.
2.
3.

HIGHLIGHT OF THE DAY

STANDOUT HUMAN OF THE DAY

SET UP FOR SUCCESS TOMORROW

day 48

POSITIVE INTENTION
Write down your positive affirmation for today.

CURRENT FEELINGS

CHOSEN FEELINGS

WHAT ARE YOU LOOKING FORWARD TO?

GOALS

I AM GRATEFUL FOR...

1.
2.
3.

Evening ☾

M　　D　　Y

OVERALL, TODAY FELT

THREE THINGS THAT WENT WELL TODAY:

1.

2.

3.

HIGHLIGHT OF THE DAY

STANDOUT HUMAN OF THE DAY

SET UP FOR SUCCESS TOMORROW

day 49

POSITIVE INTENTION
Write down your positive affirmation for today.

CURRENT FEELINGS   CHOSEN FEELINGS

WHAT ARE YOU LOOKING FORWARD TO?

GOALS

I AM GRATEFUL FOR...
1.
2.
3.

Evening ☾   M   D   Y

OVERALL, TODAY FELT

THREE THINGS THAT WENT WELL TODAY:

1. _____

2. _____

3. _____

HIGHLIGHT OF THE DAY

STANDOUT HUMAN OF THE DAY

SET UP FOR SUCCESS TOMORROW

day 50

POSITIVE INTENTION
Write down your positive affirmation for today.

CURRENT FEELINGS

CHOSEN FEELINGS

WHAT ARE YOU LOOKING FORWARD TO?

GOALS

I AM GRATEFUL FOR...

1.
2.
3.

Evening ☾

M　　D　　Y

OVERALL, TODAY FELT

THREE THINGS THAT WENT WELL TODAY:

1.
2.
3.

HIGHLIGHT OF THE DAY

STANDOUT HUMAN OF THE DAY

SET UP FOR SUCCESS TOMORROW

Build Each Other up

POSITIVITY CHALLENGE *no. 5*

PAY SOMEONE A COMPLIMENT.

Turning our focus away from ourselves and towards the people around us gives us more opportunity for joy. Give a friend a compliment today and write about how it made you feel and more importantly, how it made them feel.

DATE COMPLETED	/ /

day 51

POSITIVE INTENTION
Write down your positive affirmation for today.

CURRENT FEELINGS

CHOSEN FEELINGS

WHAT ARE YOU LOOKING FORWARD TO?

GOALS

I AM GRATEFUL FOR...

1. _____
2. _____
3. _____

Evening ☾

M   D   Y

OVERALL, TODAY FELT

THREE THINGS THAT WENT WELL TODAY:

1.
2.
3.

HIGHLIGHT OF THE DAY

STANDOUT HUMAN OF THE DAY

SET UP FOR SUCCESS TOMORROW

day 52

POSITIVE INTENTION
Write down your positive affirmation for today.

CURRENT FEELINGS

CHOSEN FEELINGS

WHAT ARE YOU LOOKING FORWARD TO?

GOALS

I AM GRATEFUL FOR...

1. _____
2. _____
3. _____

Evening ☾   M   D   Y

OVERALL, TODAY FELT

___

THREE THINGS THAT WENT WELL TODAY:

1. _____

2. _____

3. _____

HIGHLIGHT OF THE DAY

___

___

___

___

STANDOUT HUMAN OF THE DAY

___

___

SET UP FOR SUCCESS TOMORROW

day 53

POSITIVE INTENTION
Write down your positive affirmation for today.

CURRENT FEELINGS

CHOSEN FEELINGS

WHAT ARE YOU LOOKING FORWARD TO?

GOALS

I AM GRATEFUL FOR...

1. _____
2. _____
3. _____

Evening ☾

M   D   Y

OVERALL, TODAY FELT

THREE THINGS THAT WENT WELL TODAY:

1.
2.
3.

HIGHLIGHT OF THE DAY

STANDOUT HUMAN OF THE DAY

SET UP FOR SUCCESS TOMORROW

day 54

POSITIVE INTENTION
Write down your positive affirmation for today.

CURRENT FEELINGS

CHOSEN FEELINGS

WHAT ARE YOU LOOKING FORWARD TO?

GOALS

I AM GRATEFUL FOR...

1.
2.
3.

Evening ☾   M D Y

OVERALL, TODAY FELT

THREE THINGS THAT WENT WELL TODAY:

1. _____
2. _____
3. _____

HIGHLIGHT OF THE DAY

STANDOUT HUMAN OF THE DAY

SET UP FOR SUCCESS TOMORROW

day 55

POSITIVE INTENTION
Write down your positive affirmation for today.

CURRENT FEELINGS

CHOSEN FEELINGS

WHAT ARE YOU LOOKING FORWARD TO?

GOALS

I AM GRATEFUL FOR...

1.
2.
3.

Evening ☾   M   D   Y

OVERALL, TODAY FELT

THREE THINGS THAT WENT WELL TODAY:

1. _____
2. _____
3. _____

HIGHLIGHT OF THE DAY

STANDOUT HUMAN OF THE DAY

SET UP FOR SUCCESS TOMORROW

day 56

POSITIVE INTENTION
Write down your positive affirmation for today.

CURRENT FEELINGS

CHOSEN FEELINGS

WHAT ARE YOU LOOKING FORWARD TO?

GOALS

I AM GRATEFUL FOR...

1.
2.
3.

Evening ☾

M   D   Y

OVERALL, TODAY FELT

THREE THINGS THAT WENT WELL TODAY:

1.
2.
3.

HIGHLIGHT OF THE DAY

STANDOUT HUMAN OF THE DAY

SET UP FOR SUCCESS TOMORROW

day 57

 **Morning**

POSITIVE INTENTION
Write down your positive affirmation for today.

CURRENT FEELINGS

CHOSEN FEELINGS

WHAT ARE YOU LOOKING FORWARD TO?

GOALS

I AM GRATEFUL FOR...

1.
2.
3.

Evening ☾

M   D   Y

OVERALL, TODAY FELT

THREE THINGS THAT WENT WELL TODAY:

1.
2.
3.

HIGHLIGHT OF THE DAY

STANDOUT HUMAN OF THE DAY

SET UP FOR SUCCESS TOMORROW

day 58

POSITIVE INTENTION
Write down your positive affirmation for today.

CURRENT FEELINGS

CHOSEN FEELINGS

WHAT ARE YOU LOOKING FORWARD TO?

GOALS

I AM GRATEFUL FOR...

1.
2.
3.

Evening ☾   M   D   Y

OVERALL, TODAY FELT

THREE THINGS THAT WENT WELL TODAY:

1. _____

2. _____

3. _____

HIGHLIGHT OF THE DAY

STANDOUT HUMAN OF THE DAY

SET UP FOR SUCCESS TOMORROW

day 59  **Morning**

POSITIVE INTENTION
Write down your positive affirmation for today.

CURRENT FEELINGS

CHOSEN FEELINGS

WHAT ARE YOU LOOKING FORWARD TO?

GOALS

I AM GRATEFUL FOR...

1.

2.

3.

Evening ☾

M   D   Y

OVERALL, TODAY FELT

THREE THINGS THAT WENT WELL TODAY:

1. _____
2. _____
3. _____

HIGHLIGHT OF THE DAY

STANDOUT HUMAN OF THE DAY

SET UP FOR SUCCESS TOMORROW

day 60

POSITIVE INTENTION
Write down your positive affirmation for today.

CURRENT FEELINGS

CHOSEN FEELINGS

WHAT ARE YOU LOOKING FORWARD TO?

GOALS

I AM GRATEFUL FOR…

1. ___
2. ___
3. ___

Evening ☾ M D Y

OVERALL, TODAY FELT

THREE THINGS THAT WENT WELL TODAY:

1.

2.

3.

HIGHLIGHT OF THE DAY

STANDOUT HUMAN OF THE DAY

SET UP FOR SUCCESS TOMORROW

POSITIVITY CHALLENGE   *no. 6*

LEAVE YOUR PHONE IN ANOTHER ROOM FOR AN HOUR.

One of the greatest sources of daily discontentment lies in our own hands... our smart phones. Use this journal as an excuse to disconnect for a while. It can be an hour or a full day, just soak in the stillness and write about how you felt afterward.

DATE COMPLETED	/ /

60 DAY
REFLECTION

Completed on:	/	/

I feel...

I learned...

I'm proud of...

60 Things that brought me joy:

Made in the USA
Coppell, TX
15 April 2025

48318108R00085